Hers & Hers

Hers & Hers

An expression of poetry about love, loss, life
and the in between

S.L. Pannell

ISBN: 978-0-6458-3360-7

Cover by Stephanie Pannell

Illustrations by Stephanie Pannell

Gratitude flows within these pages
for every soul who danced across
the path of my heart
in this life and every life
before and after

CONTENTS

INTRODUCTION

Hers & Hers is an expression of poetry that focuses on the perspectives of two souls intimately intertwined. Both with a different view on love, life, loss and the in between. Separated into two parts, titled Mine and Hers.

The heart and mind see far beyond the eye. Our souls intuitively connect us, all the while the universe is always expressing signs to assist in growth. We must allow ourselves the opportunity to grow, to fall head over heels in love, with people, places, with life and most importantly ourselves.

Fortunately, I have spent many years surrounded by love. Giving and receiving in all shades and colours, the dark and the light. Some have even provided both at the same time.

What I have learnt, I have moved past. What lessons I have yet to conquer, I continue to face. Loving as sensitive, intense, raw, passionate and hasty as I do, being one of them. Though I would not have it any other way.

I am inspired by the memories and details from the love I have had the privilege of experiencing. With imagination, I have brought them back to life in this book.

Love always.

PART ONE:
MINE

THE FIRST DAY OF JANUARY

I question if I had ever
truly loved before you

watching you is a place
that I get lost in often
oh, how I adore you

december came and went
a perfect way to welcome
in the new year
it was a summer well spent

I never cared much for reading
until you surprised me with a book
it was about past life connections
and then you gave me that look

on the first day of january
when the dawn broke through

you did not have to confess
I could see it in your eyes
you had fallen in love too

SUN KISSED SKIN

Home to me
was not four walls
and a roof above my head

it was sun kissed skin
brown eyes
home was with you instead

UNCHARTED

We get lost in one another
I use your body as a map

though my hands may wander
when they begin to tire
they fall effortlessly into your lap

the backstreets of your neck
my lips know them well
your river runs wild
as you begin to swell

the same river I've dipped in
since that night in december
lost in one another
then suddenly we remember

that this land is uncharted
a love like ours was not made
for the faint-hearted

THE SUNSET DRESS

Her dress looked like
the most beautiful sunset
my eyes had ever witnessed

I am sure I was not alone
when I say that the whole room
could almost taste her
on the tip of their tongues

she has that way with people
a breath of fresh air for your lungs

but it is me that she comes home to
I am the lucky one
who slides off her sunset dress

leaving my soul completely full
and our hotel room a mess

THE GREAT ESCAPE

You came as soft
as you spoke
as soft as the kisses
in the morning
as soon as we woke

in my mind
you take me places
I have yet to see

with your hands
you take me from
the bed to belize

the sound of your voice
I go weak at the knees

we travel together
in these fine moments
the world is at our feet

our eyes explore
one another
and finally
they meet

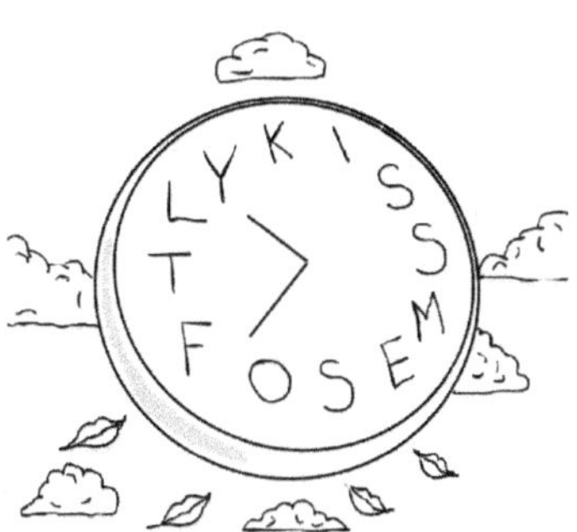

TIMELESS

If I had a favourite memory
it is how you would make
a bed out of my body

the left side was yours
a safe place to lay
without any worry

I would hold you for hours
and we would stare at the sky

a feeling I could never explain
though I never wondered why

we worshipped the sunsets
as if it were our religion

the whole world moved around us
time was never wasted
it was a sweet disposition

THE HEALING

You looked good in anything
or simply nothing at all

every time you stepped out of the shower
I begged for the towel to fall

it was the method of undressing you
understanding the science behind
the placement of my hands whilst
caressing you

something I could never unlearn
in fact, I only wanted to know more

I kiss all your insecurities
and run my fingers across any flaw

together we heal parts of us
that no lover from the past has before

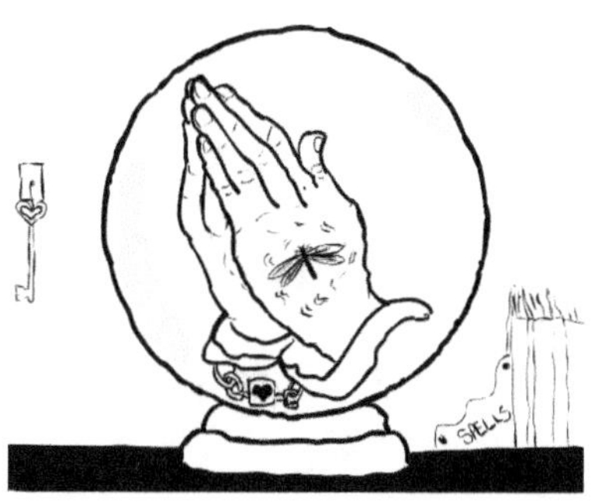

HEART OF GOLD

Your favourite scent was freshly cut grass
and mine a blown-out candle

demons in your mind
though there was nothing that I couldn't handle

I don't think anyone ever held you as you cried
or comforted you in the cold

some stared straight through you
yet I saw a heart made of gold

I hope that one day you will learn your worth
and that you learn it long before you ever leave this earth

MARY JANE

Her smile when she raises her eyebrow
forces you to forget everything
except the here and now

her presence is a present
as we lay in bed with mary jane

with nothing but our minds to lose
and a whole lot to gain

I stay for a while here on cloud nine
she lays her body across me
calling herself *mine*

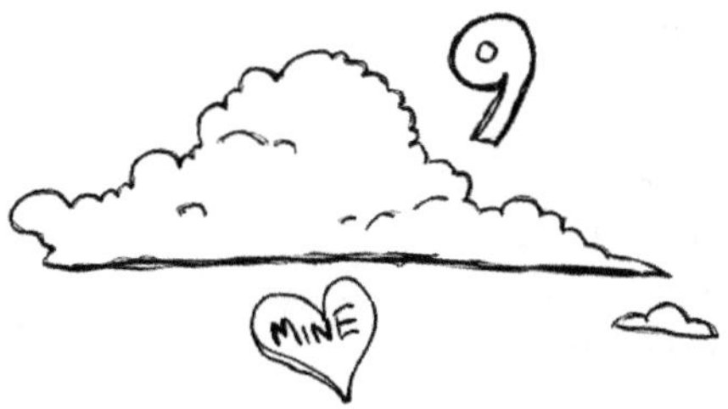

IN THE CLOUDS

Gravity ceases to exist
whenever you are in view
I would move time and space
just to lay here for a
moment longer with you

somewhere in the clouds
where we lose sight of the ground
with just you and I
no one else around

give me every detail
of your life before me
how you earned that scar
and the story behind it
as we drive in your parent's car

paint the picture of your first kiss
in your small hometown
which is everything you ran from
now suddenly you miss

the home you took your first steps in
still covered in snow
share stories with me about it
in the afternoon glow

pull back the sheets to the bed
that you laid in at seventeen
give me every detail about your
love, life, loss and the in between

CINNAMON AND HONEY

She smelt like cinnamon and honey
and spent more time at work than home
but did not do it for the money

she made plans to travel the world
and did it on her own
I am proud of her heart
for how much it had grown

she avoided love but tempted lust
a heart locked away entirely
until she met eyes she could trust

eyes warm and blue
they hold her for hours
cinnamon and honey
oh, the sweet smell of you

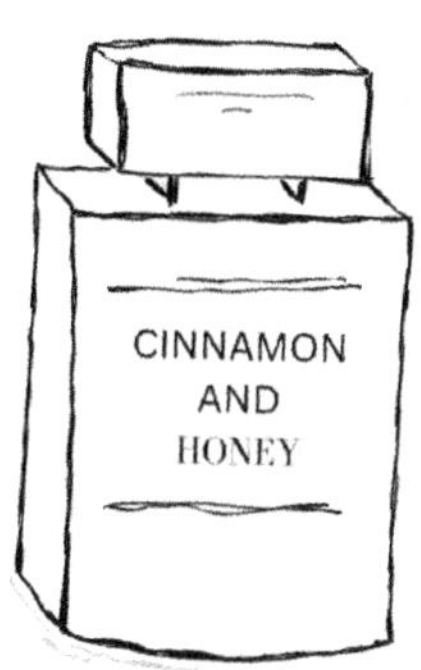

OURS AND HOURS

What is yours is mine
mine is yours
together it is ours

I live for days like this
sun setting beyond
the mountains
we call this
the golden hours

a strong posture
we sit beneath the trees
sharing gentle kisses
between the ones from
the ocean breeze

our bodies intertwined
I forget who is who
we forget ourselves in the process
it is just what lovers do

but what is mine is yours
yours is mine
same souls
only different bodies
in every life time

DARLING

Teasing me with her skin
covered in red lace
the warning before impact
I begin to brace

I have no doubt that
flying also feels like falling
strong eye contact
with a corner smile
I sense her body calling

she knows me personally
though never calls me
by my name

she has been referring
to me as *darling*
since the night we met

and I have never been
the same

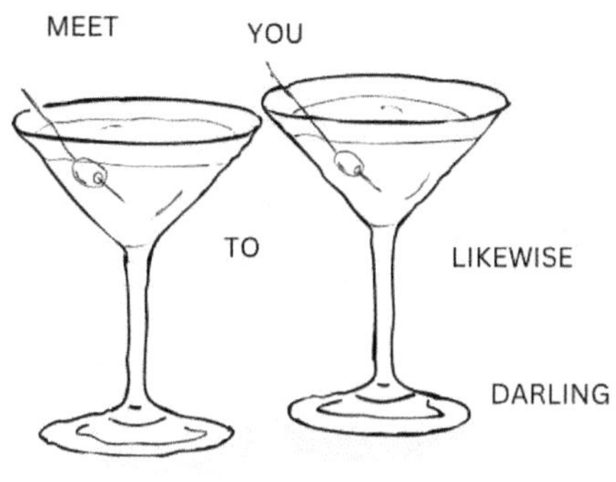

THE CHAUFFER

In the kitchen
she kisses the middle
of my back

speaks two or
three words
then my mind
runs off track

she traces the outlines
of my body
with the softness
of her gaze

hands that felt
like fire
and legs that
went on for days

I ask her politely
where she would
like me to take her

I offer the counter
the walls, floors
and the sofa

I would take her anywhere
she calls me her chauffer

MASTERPIECE

I watch her
take nothing
then turn it
into something

a steady hand
yet a fragile heart

it was not the paint
on the canvas
to me
you were the art

the concentration
on your face
the patience
of your hands
when you draw

I sit in silence
you have no idea
my mind and body
are in complete awe

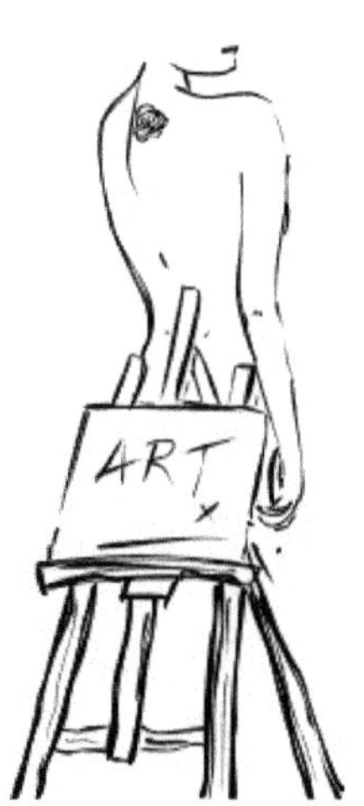

HOME

Morning light comes creeping in
soft blankets and softer kisses

you are warm to touch
and your body is calling me home

a place for my head to rest
land for my hands to roam

CHERRY WINE

Go wild on me
those are the words
she led with
once her lips had left mine

those words
they age so well
like the finest
drop of cherry wine

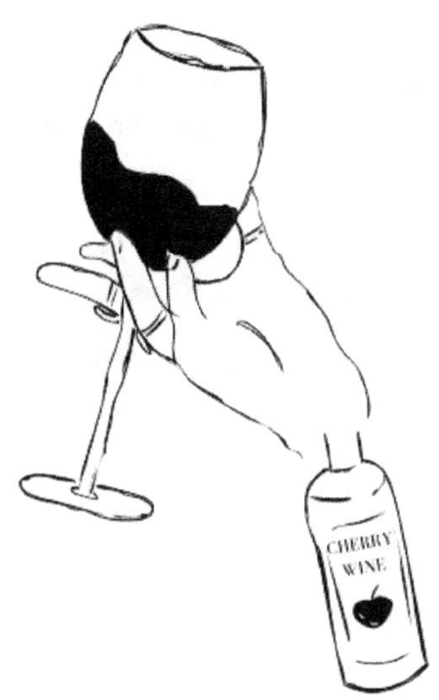

LIPS MADE OF INK

Guide my hands down your spine
allow me to open you in the centre

at the very heart of your book
I held your eyes in the moment
so I never forget that look

running my fingertips over paragraphs
that force you to gasp for air

I only fold the corners of my favourite pages
just so you are aware

I press the ink on my lips against your skin
you take a deep breath then grasp my hand
to invite me in

we finish the book together
an ending that will leave your lungs breathless
with a final moan

thoughts for her to ponder over
on nights that she is bare skin and alone

A WILD RIDE

I already had my license
though she taught me
how to drive

to speed through
her valleys and hills
a rush where
I felt most alive

she taught me how to
keep one eye on the road
and one on her

one hand on the wheel
the other on her thigh
how I prefer

I learnt how to kiss her
at every red light
and take off on the green

she taught me
how to navigate by the
constellations of stars
and what each of them mean

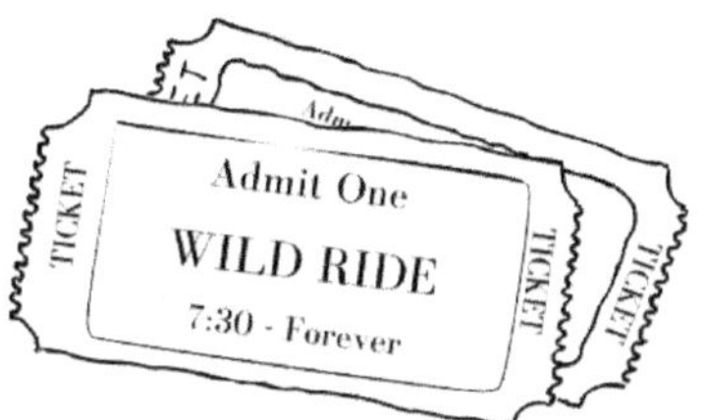

reverse and parallel
I mastered each park
I learnt how to find her
lips in the light
and again in the dark

BLACK AND WHITE

I take pictures of her
with her smile always ear to ear by the ocean

away from the city lights
and all the commotion

the contrast of the waves against the midnight sky
black and white

her body the most beautiful shade of both
as she is kissed gradually by moonlight

she takes my hand after a heavy conversation
leading me towards the waves
with no need for persuasion

once her clothes fall from her body onto the sand
I step back to take her all in
she fit perfectly into the palm of my hand

MY SHIRT

You look like the definition of magic
how I caved from a single glance of you
was nothing short of tragic

as you move across the room in nothing
except my oversized shirt

a subtle way of displaying intimacy
I discover that this is how you flirt

I lay with a coffee in hand
you dance for me from a distance

the rest of the world ceases to exist
in this very instance

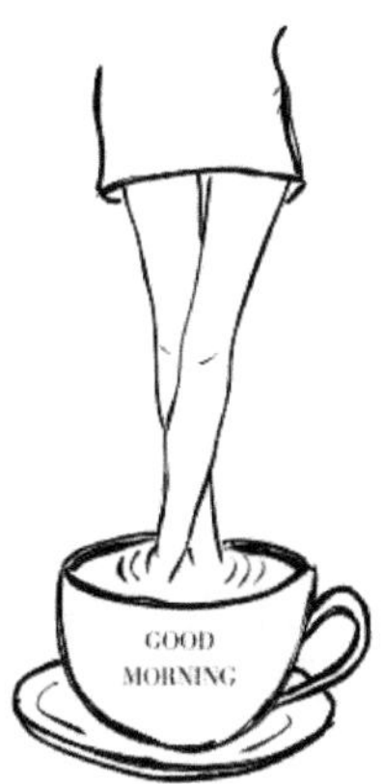

GONE GIRL

Heights, tight spaces
and carnival rides
were never the problem
the thought of losing you
became my greatest fear

it is as if I spent a lifetime
searching for you
then somehow
we did survive another year

I find peace in knowing
that perhaps you were never
truly mine to keep

and comfort knowing
you exist vividly in dreams
of mine when I sleep

THE AFTERMATH

That night on the beach
a blanket and red wine
as you rest in arm's reach

we exchange words
in hope for closure
as soon as they are spoken
I barely keep my composure

I can count on one hand
how many times I have
witnessed you cry
tears stream down your cheek
during the unwanted goodbye

you take a piece of my heart
when you stand to leave
though you did not have
to search far and wide
it had been there all along
on the edge of my sleeve

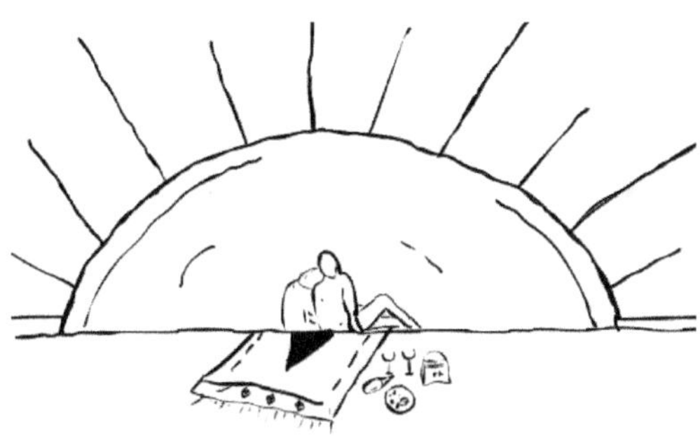

GHOST OF YOU

I adore you, she says
and *I only want the best*

a letter goodbye
is an ending I would
never have guessed

empty promises
and an empty bed

all you left behind
once you fled

I still feel you here
roaming the halls
of my mind
like a ghost

tell me how
do you let go
of the one
you want the most

LOST ANGELS

I was screaming her name
in the middle of the street
I was in the city of LA
speaking of her to strangers
as if they had plans to meet

I spoke of her heart
how I made a home out of it
right from the start

some looked at me crazy
others in vain
like they knew anything
about her love
and how without it
I feel insane

I plead with myself
as well as family and friends
swearing truthfully
that our love knew no ends

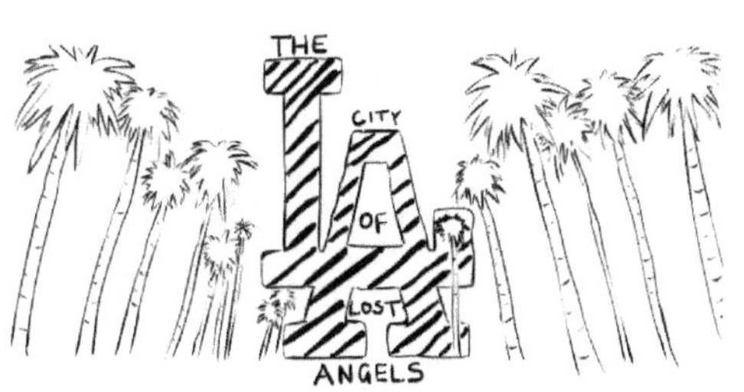

DISTANCE

A hopeless romantic
I surrender at the thought
there are lessons to be learnt
through lovers they will be taught

forgiving you was my deadliest sin
though I was never one for games
losing you was my biggest win

time went on and
the distance begun
all I wanted was for you stay
so, why did you run

breadcrumbs of conversation
you would always suck me in
tear drops fall heavy
on this roof made of tin

THE WORDS LEFT UNSAID

Unassured and insecure
I have many flaws
though I wish I had fewer
a cinema of trauma
where I am the sole viewer

you had your wounds too
you never completely healed
the anxiety and depression

perhaps we never do
though with you
there was always suppression

the things we never did
or words we never said

the silence is louder
than ever as we lay
side by side in our bed

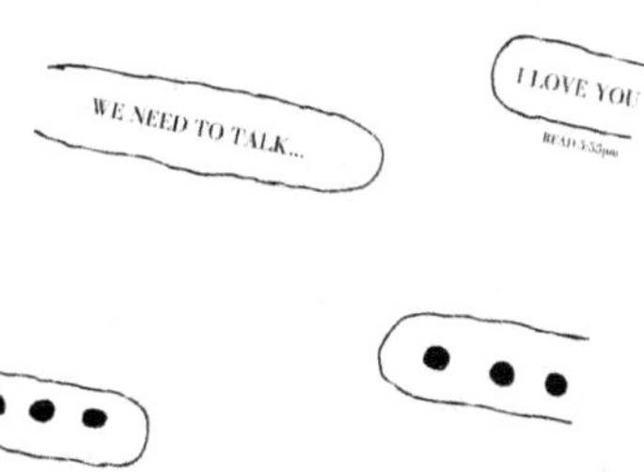

THE MOON

Darling, I have spent countless nights
howling at the moon
and there are things that I share with him
that I wish I could have with you

in between the heavy sighs
cries and endless whys
he whispers
at least you have known love

consoling words spoken
from the wise man above
as some have never allowed
their hearts to be open

in that moment, I am reminded
that not everything
in this world is built to last

some things we grasp onto
then some we graze with our fingertips
as they effortlessly flow past

a colourful museum of our love and arts
remanence of memories
shared between two hearts

there are splashes of red
and shades of blue
things that will remind you of me
and I of you

there will be places we go
and places we don't
for reasons, we do
and for reasons we won't

as dusk turns to dawn
I realise that
beneath the moon
is the safest place to mourn

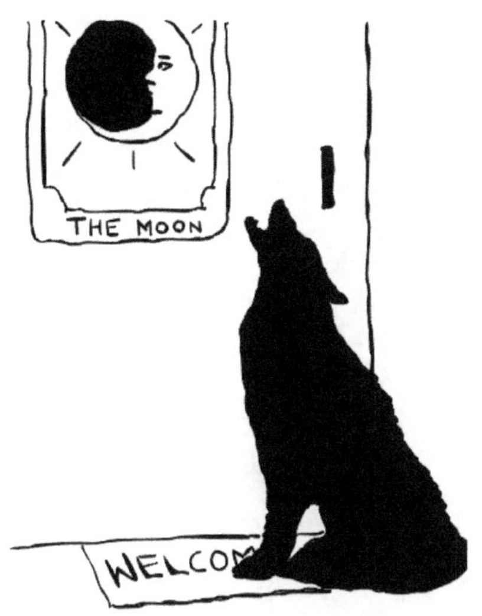

ME

I was loving you and losing me
it was subtle and sweet

not one before the other
it was simultaneously

HEARTBREAK HOTEL

There is passion in pain
and pain in passion

you sip red wine
while my hands are wrapped around
the glass of an old fashioned

we discuss the future and plans that we will make
what was intended to be a holiday
felt solely of heart ache

I shattered into a million pieces
barely allowing myself to breathe

there is only enough room
here for one of us to grieve

so pack your bags
and run baby run

you pulled the trigger
though I handed you the gun

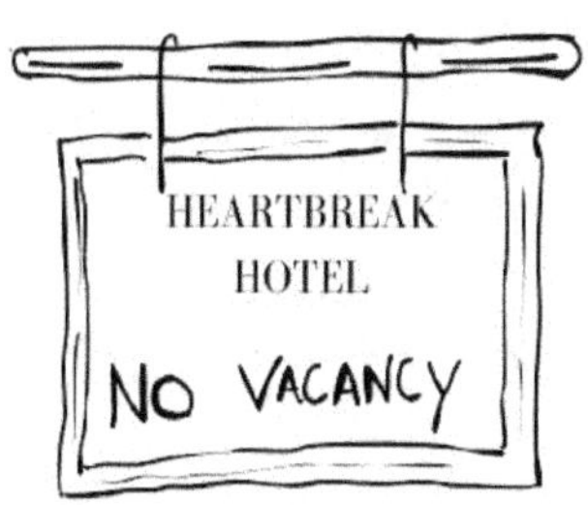

THOSE EYES

A soulmate, karmic partner or a twin flame
they each come in disguise

if not this life, then another
I hope you give me those eyes

we find each other again
perhaps a café, the beach
or a sunflower field

this time is different
this time we are healed

you still play with your hair
the strands of it behind your ear

I still whisper, *I love you*
just loud enough for you to hear

a nostalgic feeling
that we have met before
as our clothes fall like autumn leaves
onto your bedroom floor

HINDSIGHT

One day you will look back
and it does not hurt quite as much

begging for the bare minimum
yearning for a compliment or
some form of physical touch

things that should have come naturally
you will know when you get there

the feeling of no longer bitter
for you did not give up on love
you were never the quitter

SUNFLOWERS

From time to time
I wonder about the necklace
that I draped around you
the last time we had met

I wonder if it still rests perfectly
below the bones of your neck

parts of you I wish to kiss
parts of you I will always miss

what about the sunflowers
have you thrown them out

in fact, tell me nothing
leave room for me to doubt

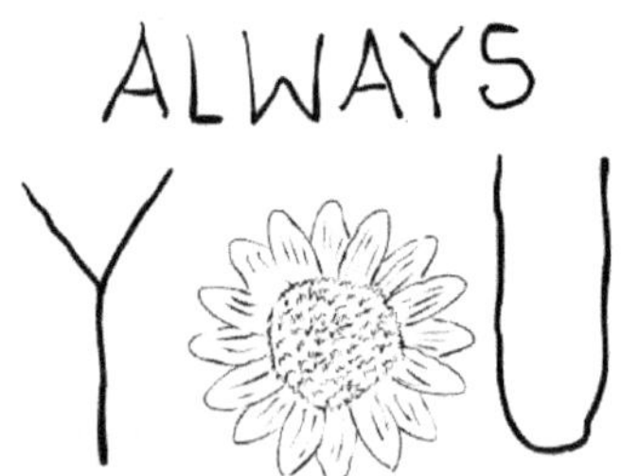

WHEN YOU ARE READY

Time heals all wounds
well, so they say
you may not completely understand it
not in the thick of it anyway

one day you will wake up
and it all makes perfect sense

you no longer speak about them
in present or future
only in past tense

the true demons are not found
under your bed
despite what you have heard
they exist in your mind instead

you cannot make a home there
you must come and go

take comfort in the uncertainty
through the ebb and flow

BITING THE BULLET

She asked for some time to heal from things
that she had never felt
this is the gamble that we take with love
these are the cards I have been dealt

she plants a kiss on my forehead
then sends me on my way
as if leaving was my choice
when I begged her to stay

I gather my things and leave with little pride
careful to step over the puddle of tears
from where we had cried

there is a bullet that we must bite
when the flame no longer burns how it used to
and we can no longer keep it alight

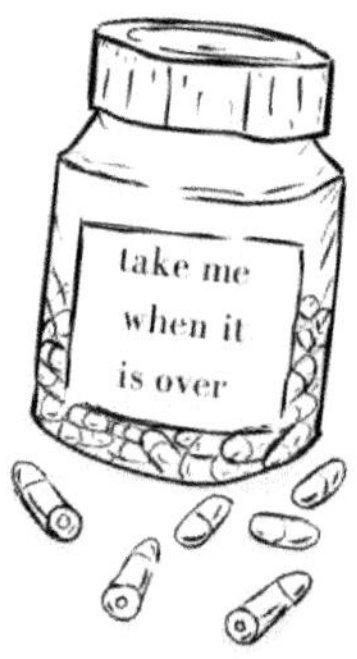

LESSONS AND BLESSINGS

She taught me a lot
challenged me more
than anyone before

she taught me how to talk
to avoid conflict and deter
she taught me how to walk
slow and barefoot like her

she changed with the seasons
without any explanation
she fell short of reasons

we never saw this coming
but truth be told
I felt like you never had the visions
of the two of us growing old

did anyone ever tell you
that it is not about the
sticks and stones

it is the words that break me
they shattered my confidence
and all of my bones

I learn how to self-soothe
then pick myself up
I learn how to love myself first
before pouring from an empty cup

BOUND TO YOU

I thought I was ready
to share the sheets
with someone new

in the morning
when I woke
my hands went
searching for you

the body of yours
that I never found

rumour has it
that in exchange for love
our souls will always be bound

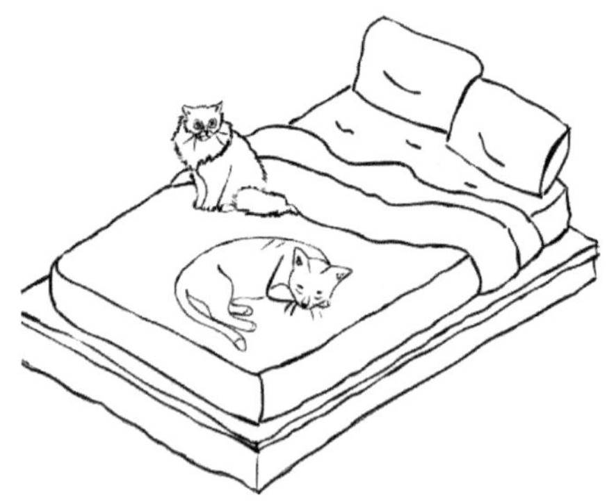

BLUE BIRD

Your hands were full of
seven cards and each finger
housed crystal rings

someone once told me
when you die, you hear the
blue bird as it sings

I heard them that night
we laid by the river

they saw the look in my eyes
the way my lip revealed a quiver

the end was near as soon
as you said the words

my heart fell through my chest
as my mind flocked
with a thousand blue birds

MY HANDS

These hands are mine
though if I listen closely
they call for you

my heart used to
flush with red
and now it runs blue

the numbing pains
that seep through
all my arteries
and into my veins

a constant reminder
of a love that turned cold

these hands are mine
but for you my love
they will always fold

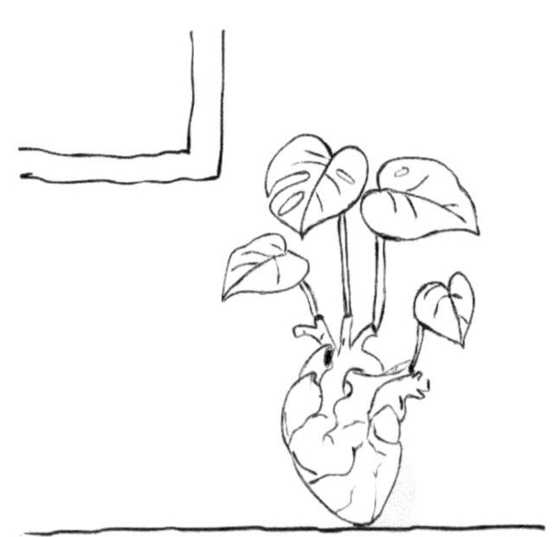

INSOMNIA

Staring at the ceiling
I lay awake in attempts
to count sheep

my tired eyes and heart
could do with some sleep

love has never been easy
it is the furthest thing from fair
I confide in the silence
though I find no comfort there

what happened to all is fair
in love and war
I retreat to darkness
licking wounds
that are still raw

I want to run to you and hide between
your skin and the sheets

you do not need to say a word
let us speak in a language
understood by only our heart beats

ULTRA-NOSTALGIA

It is as if your lips and mine
are dear old friends meeting again
for the first time

my hands are tucked
on either side of your jaw

endless kisses somehow
still leave me wanting more

dear old friends
now brand new

you whisper how you have missed this
oh, how I have too

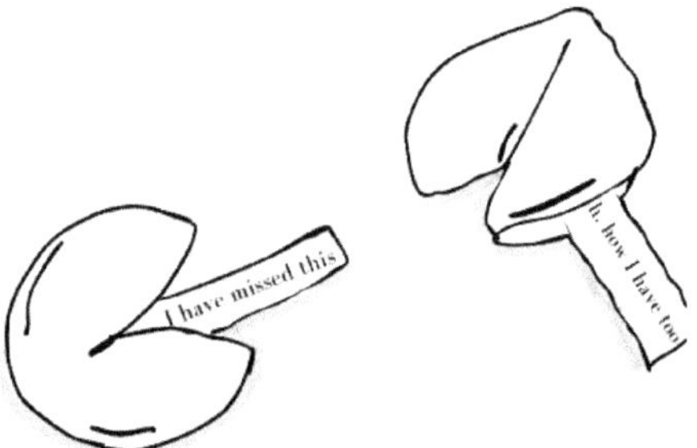

THE THIEF

I lose track of the time
how the dark steals the light
should be considered a crime

some days our skies are blue
then there are some with only grey
we argue over stupid things
usually over the words that I say

hurting you is never my intention
I go back to what I know
as if I use it as protection

my heart has not only been bruised
but it has been broken
the scars that sleep
under this skin of mine
have finally woken

you teach me to breathe deep
think about the words
before they are spoken
before the damage is done
before the wounds reopen

I am the student and you are the master
there are triggers in actions
as soon as you disappear
it forces my heart to beat faster

WHEN I MISS YOU

I revisit you
in slow songs
photographs
and the ocean

a poetic
expression
of my love
and devotion

when I miss you
there are places
I go to feel you close

the unexpected
goodbyes
are the ones
that always
seem to hurt
the most

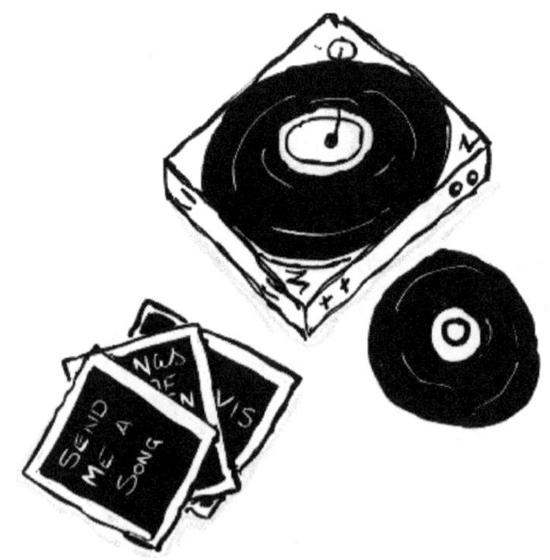

MEMOIR

Loving you made me a better person
I now know when to let go
and when to hold on tighter

losing you felt like grieving the living
each day felt like a funeral
however, it made me a better writer

YOU

If they ever ask about you, this is what I will say:
she felt like all four seasons in one day

her morning coffee
was black and barely warm

they warn you about her
the calm before the storm

she worked long shifts
then slept until noon

she danced in the sun
and surrendered to the moon

the sweetest kisses and the softest touch
she did not beg for anything
in fact, she never asked for much

she thought her eyes were lifeless
up close they looked like mars

ironically, our first kiss was shared
under a handful of shooting stars

it was way past late
what was meant to be one drink
turned into a five hour first date

she could feel free
and trapped at the same time
a balancing act
and she walked a fine line

she smelt like the ocean
and pulled you in with the tide
she was once in a lifetime
one hell of a ride

PART TWO:
HERS

GALAXY EYES

Somewhere lost in translation
the whole world went silent
as if it were only for our conversation

we spoke a little about life
shared our stories with the moon and stars

I was a homebody and strayed far from the bars
she was an old soul with a mind so wise

suddenly the stars left the night sky
and begun dancing in her eyes

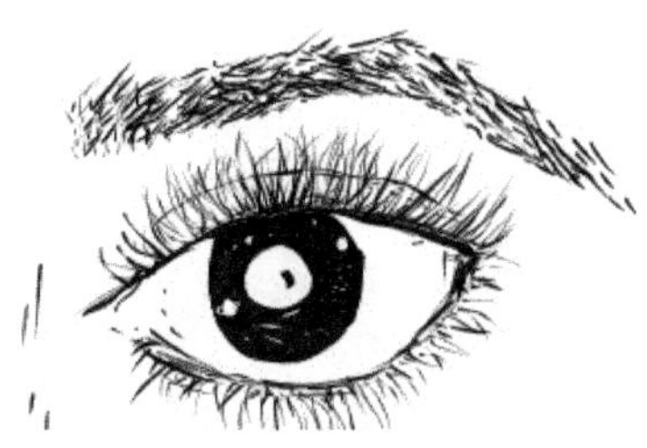

DIVINE TIMING

Who do you think you are
walking into my life unapologetically
giving those blue eyes from afar

praising you for being bold and brave
I have never felt so drawn to someone
although I will take that to the grave

who do you think you are
walking into my life
when the timing was divine

becoming completely infatuated with you
over a shared bottle of orange wine

A DIFFERENT LIGHT

I see you, you see me
we learn to see each other
in different lights, respectfully

I don't dare change you
or pull you apart at your core

I learn to love every fibre of you
including every flaw

to me there are few
to you there are many more

these are what makes you human
and the human that I adore

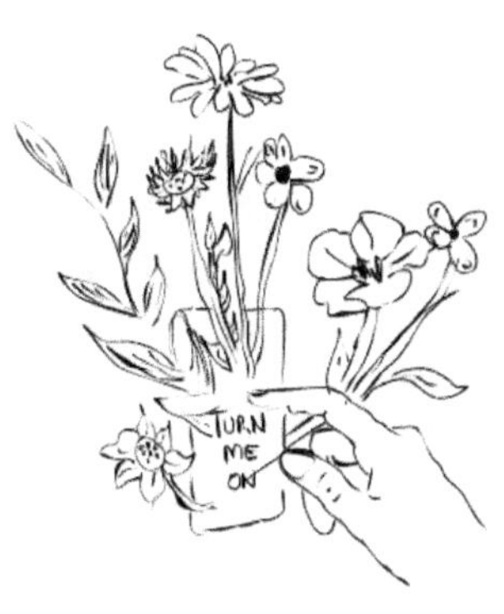

A COLLECTABLE

The heart of yours
that beats beneath your chest
is yours and yours only

remember that on the nights
you feel overwhelmed and lonely

you are one of a kind
a collector's item
a rare find

you begin to realise
people do not love
the way that you do

though I would spend
a lifetime searching
for a rarity like you

THE BIRDS AND THE BEES

Insatiable and tempting
almost hard to resist
there is always love
here with you and
never a closed fist

you take my hand
lead me from
the sand to the shore
my body a land
you so eagerly explore

my legs wrap
around your waist
like vines on the trees

as we rewrite the story
about the birds
and the bees

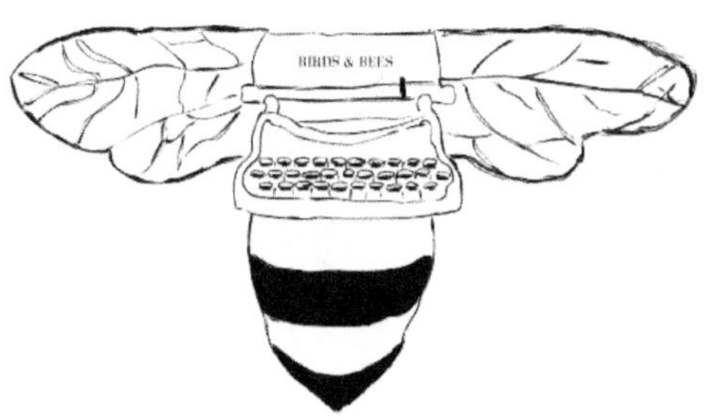

ON THE ROCKS

An angel when she is in front of company
then subtly shifts to a devil in my backseat

asking if I *prefer my whiskey on the rocks*
or *prefer my whiskey neat*

lounging over me like I am
a piece of furniture in her living room

I worship her body
and the sweet smell of her perfume

her hands run over my back
then linger on me for hours

she sends shivers down my spine
and they spread like wildflowers

SURRENDER

There is something
that you hold over me
when you are under me

I surrender myself to you
with absolute certainty

this may not last forever
maybe it is just for tonight

until now, I was never
a firm believer in
love at first sight

when your eyes held mine
it was as if the universe
worked its magic
summoning the stars to align

THE RABBIT AND THE HARE

Slow and steady
that is how I wish to embrace your love
like something you have longed to uncover

independence is something I yearn for
not only what I desire in a lover

I need time and space to truly miss you
save your love letters and midnight calls
I need you to entirely disappear out of view

it is not that I do not love you
you see, it is because I do

SUNDAY MORNINGS

Hair long, medium brown, with gentle curls
that are barely touching the skin on your back

you tower your torso above me
balancing on my waist, you are quite the act

I swear the ink of your tattoos are moving to your breath
drop your head and aim for the clouds

we remain in our sanctuary on sunday morning
avoiding the crowds

sing out in that angelic voice and call me *baby*
could we do this again next sunday
or for forever, maybe

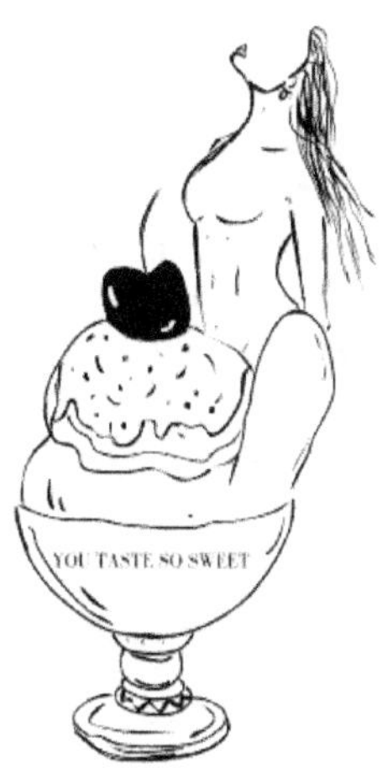

HER ROOTS

Run your fingers through my hair
simply soften these edges
if you dare

breathe soft and slow
your energy is magnetic
our chemistry close to overflow

revealing your shadows in the mirror on the ceiling
you fold majestically to sound
gifting me with the vision of you and I
making love on the ground

careful with your mouth
as you explore my neck with your lips
before smooth sailing south

exposing your hard truths
in your darkest hours
using sex as your exchange for love
you never cared for flowers

they taught you to pose like a trophy on their shelf
I harvest your roots out of the ground
and teach you to love yourself

SLIDING DOORS

There are moments
where I fall in love with you all over again

you are laughing with your friends
or how you comfort me
and reassure me that all bad days have ends

when you talk about something passionately
or share with me
your hopes and dreams

you have been the greatest motivation
to dive in headfirst
no matter how shallow the water seems

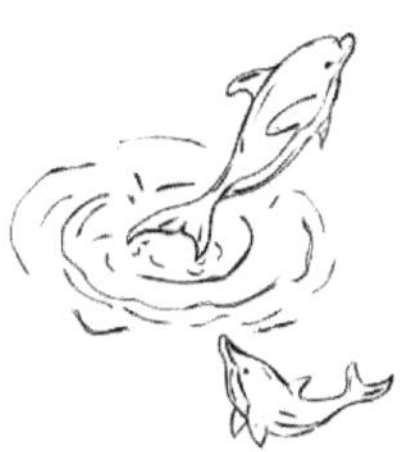

AQUARIUS

She bathes in sunlight
as it calls her body home
she won't blend well into crowds
take her somewhere she feels most alone

but don't leave just yet
watch her from afar
allow her to release her
bottled up emotions
when you loosen her jar

she fumbles her words
and loses her train of thought

take her into the wild
and let her run as if
she fears being caught

eventually she will turn to you
and thank you for simply being there
because loving her freely
is proving to her how much you truly care

SEASHELLS

Our footsteps in the sand
clarity and peace fill my mind
as we walk hand in hand

we admire the seashells
but we never take them home
it was nothing we agreed upon together
we came up with it on our own

we considered removing them
was all about possession
so we leave them where they are
and appreciate without obsession

strange for a stranger to think
exactly like you
perhaps we aren't really strangers
and we discussed the seashells
in another life or perhaps a few

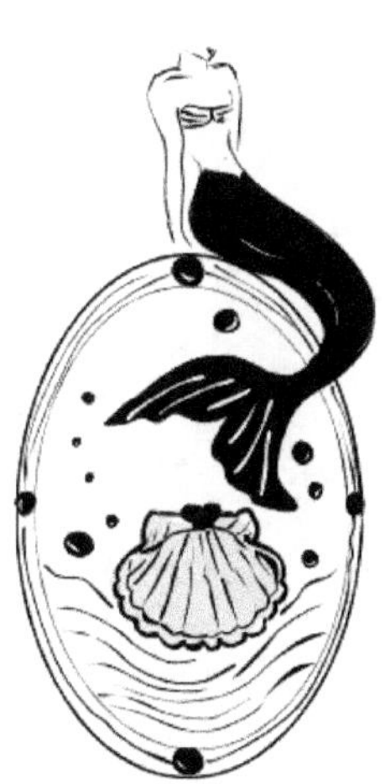

BLUE

Her pupils surrounded with gold and blue
I adore them once they dilate
whenever she declares *I love you*

now that I have had the privilege of holding them
I don't think I will ever look at another's the same

those blue eyes hang from my wall
next to mine, in a frame

certain that I will still love them
long after the last time that I ever call her name

WATERFALLS

Whenever we get tired of the real world
we disappear into nature
beneath the trees and waterfalls

she studies my skin and soul here
gentle and soft when she breaks down my walls

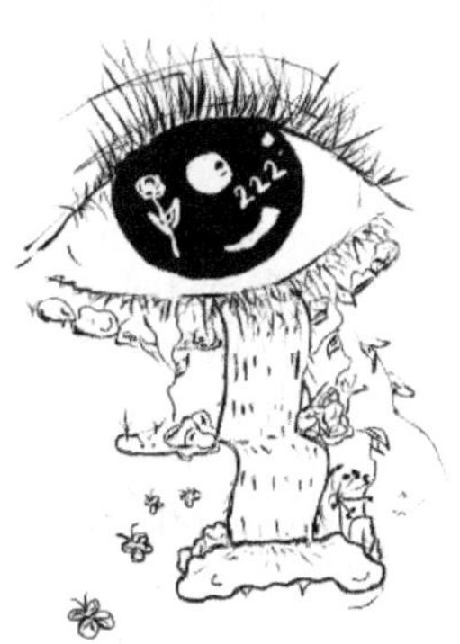

this is close to something that I am needing
to repair the damage other bodies have done
her words stop the bleeding

away from everything I have ever known
even in a crowded room
she has a way of making me feel
like we are entirely alone

reading her poetry out loud
as if the words on the pages were written for me
waterfalls stream down my face
every single one of them she says promisingly

ANGEL NUMBERS

The universe challenges me every once in a while
in the little signs and signals
and through the brunette with the golden smile

hand delivered to send me a lesson
to teach me what I have failed to learn
about healing without suppression

repeating numbers on the clock and license plate
keep me believing that we met for a reason
not by chance, but instead by fate

convinced she is an angel that has fallen from heaven
she is both everywhere and nowhere
I notice the time is 11:11

LINGER A WHILE LONGER

Smoke me like one of your french cigarettes
when I light up and you draw me in

I fill your apartment with my scent
it is embedded into your skin

we make love in the afternoons
and as I cook dinner, you linger

how you are perched on the counter
I realise you wrapped around my finger

then I overstay my welcome
by more than a few days

your body a temple
but darling, your mind is a maze

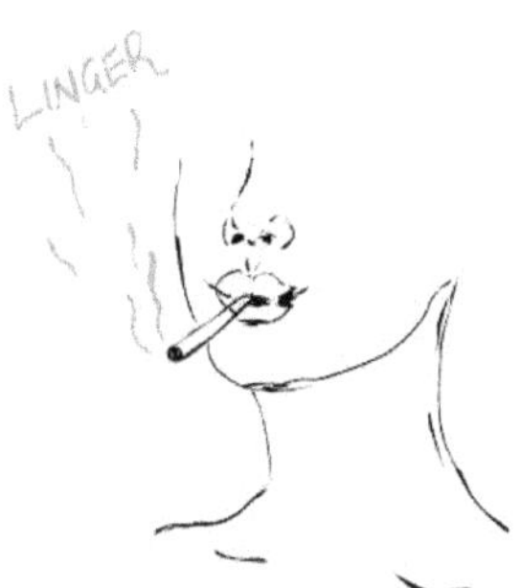

THE SUN

I envy the sun
how she is able
to kiss you
before I do

how she shines
her morning light
on you and turns
the sky the most
beautiful shade
of blue

she could do
more for you
than I ever could

perhaps that is
untrue
and just more
than I ever would

even though
I love you
I will let you go
it is just
what I do

a fear of
commitment
a fear of
hurting you

WHEN I LEAVE

She craves my affection
my love and constant attention
for a sense of security and protection

the little things that seem simple
I fold the corners of her heart
allowing the rest of it to crimple

a kiss on the forehead
she irons out the creases

when I leave, I am full
and she is in pieces

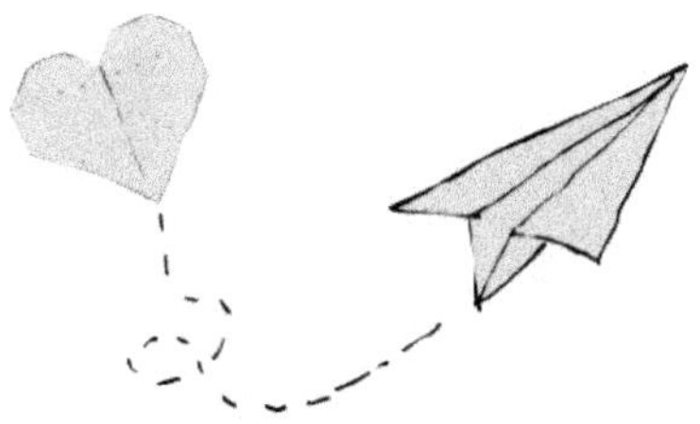

IF ONLY

You play effortlessly with the chemicals in my brain
the push and pull of your arms
you send me out into the wilderness
and then call my name

I do not walk
I run back to you
I have been warned
but only if they knew

you play me like your guitar strings
the push and pull of your voice
as you speak
not to mention when it sings

I do not run
I walk away from you
if only I listened
if only I knew

UNREQUITED LOVE

There are things
that we will never know

things I will never tell you
things I will never show

I hold my emotions close on the inside
I never learnt how to comfort you
or to truly confide

it is simple that way if I do not give you
my heart then I will not get hurt

I do not want to leave you
and I do not want to sleep in the dirt

I will call you when I want you
then disappear soon after

you can disguise your tears around me
and trade them for laughter

FIRE AND COAL

There are days I wake up
and convince myself
you will leave me tomorrow

and if you did my world would fill
of longing and sorrow

but for some reason you stay
suddenly my skies are no longer grey

you put the colour back
inside of my world

in the golden hour
and the loose curls in your hair
from where your fingers had twirled

I have an epiphany that I don't
want to spend my dawns and dusks
with any other soul

even though there are days I wake up
no longer walking on eggshells
instead I walk on fire and coal

convincing myself that you will
leave me tonight

sacrificing my own needs to
make this all right

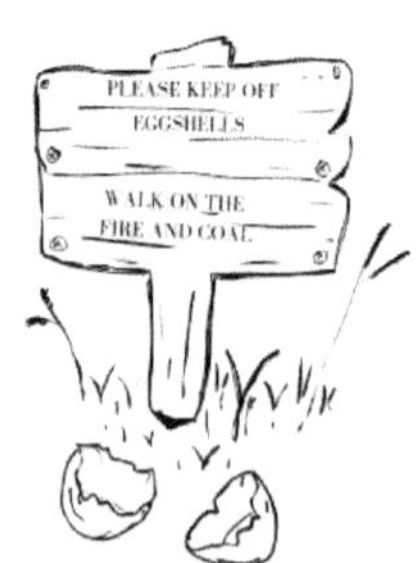

US

I asked her in a moment
of sheer desperation
how she got over her and I

she said she never did
then held her breath
to save the cry

this is where I become
completely confused

I never got over you
the lines are blurred

the most heartbreaking
yet beautiful words
that I had ever heard

DIVERSIONS

I distract myself
with little white lines
and bottles of liquor
I can barely pronounce

ingested into my body
the places I have not felt in years
consumed in deadly amounts

the bodies that come and go from my bed
help drown out the last words that she said

when I lay still, they echo
though I am loosely holding on
it hurts me more to let go

BRAVE

It is a pattern
I have learnt how to wade
uncomfortable in her waters

they learn to love like you do
so be kind to your daughters

sometimes her waters are calm
more often than not
they are unpredictable and rough

somehow, I brave them
but somehow brave
still is not brave enough

FREE

She was a prisoner in her own mind
I was down on my hands and knees
searching for something within her
something I would never find

breaking my own heart thinking
I won't be around to see those eyes
how they will wither and change
as the time flies

the fact my hands will find a new place to rest
when they have been yours for so long now
your lap was home to them
some kind of a nest

they pass over cities and lakes
eventually they learnt to fly on their own
all the while I hold onto hope they return
to the only home, they have ever known

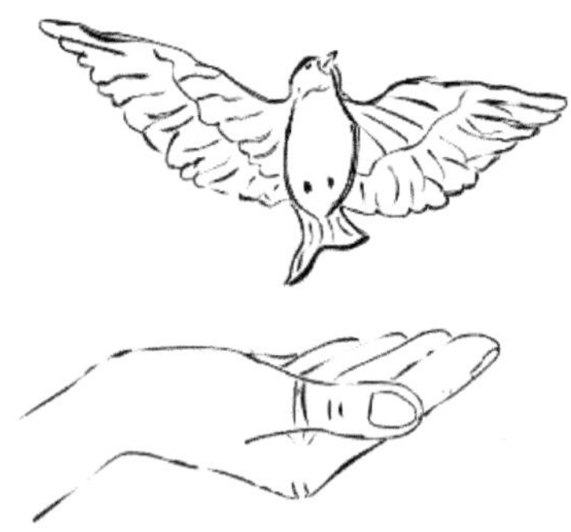

THE SADDEST PART

Ignorance is bliss
erasing any thought of you with someone else
just so I can keep those lips to kiss

pretending I don't smell the scent of their cologne
and I ensure I smile politely
as you tell me, you spent your nights alone

how are we supposed to make our love last
when you spend your days
with a lover from your past

the saddest part, is they know about me
they know I am trying desperately

so, will you sit me down
and break my heart delicately

say *it's not you, it's me*
hold my hand and look me in the eyes

tug on the strings of my intuition
to warn me they're lies

MY SAILOR

She sailed the seven seas
I sailed them in her eyes
they filled with tears
as I said my goodbyes

dark to light blue
they change when you cry
please don't come
looking for me
don't ever wonder why

I shy from my emotions
don't you dare ponder me
as you set sail across
the oceans

if it is meant to be
whisper you love me
and then set me free

if I ever come back
then I am yours to keep

I may be built of armour
but alone is when I weep

if I never do
speak to me through
the lyrics of our song

it may not have always felt right
but it was never wrong

no matter where we are
in the world
we will always share
the same moon

maybe you and I
share the same thought
did we give up too soon

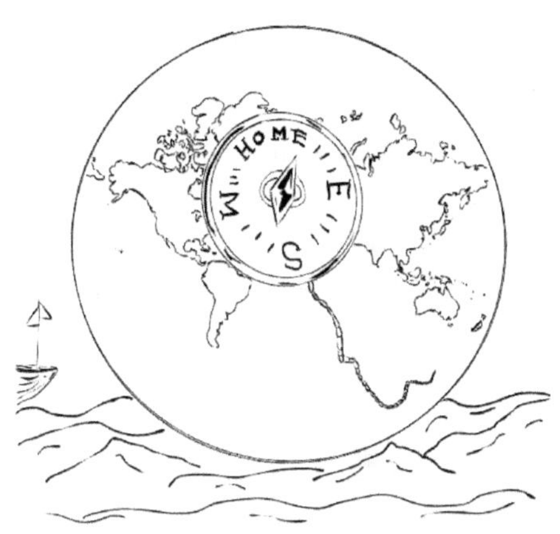

COCAINE VEIN

Her love keeps me up through the night
indulging in her as if she were lines of cocaine

her voice soothes my soul
just like the midnight rain

if I was given a little more time
I could have loved you better

if you never read the words out loud
in that handwritten letter

keep me living in dreams
that play like movies inside of my head

love me to death
then bring me back from the dead

and do it over and over again
rip my soul from my bones

your silhouette dances with mine
I am mesmerised by their shades and tones

her love keeps me up all through the night
a fleeting love and she is nowhere in sight

if I was given a little more time
I could have loved you better

if you never read the words out loud
in that handwritten letter

NOW AND THEN

Imagine never understanding the depths of love
I don't mean what you are used to
I am talking about the bottom of the earth and up above

have you ever felt your own heart break when you see her cry
or do you stand back and ask her questions, such as *why*

did you chase her when she walked slowly out your door
or were her footsteps not loud enough to shake you at your core

when my blood spills, it spells your name
imagine finally understanding the depths of love
and they no longer feel the same

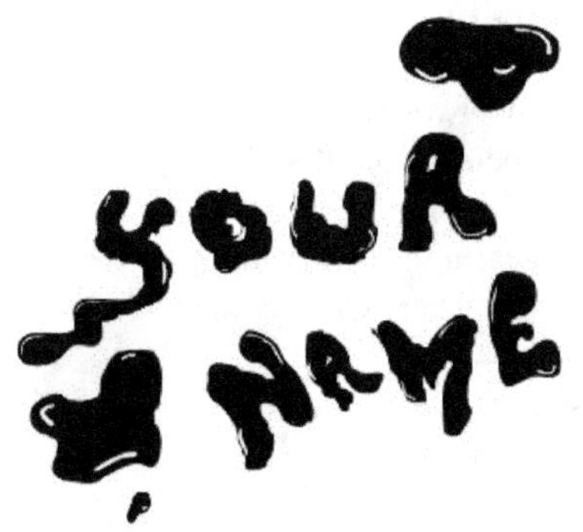

HOPE IS A HEARTACHE

Now that it is over
this is the kind of heartbreak
that drains the tears from your eyes
and leaves you completely sober

you never left a bitter taste on my tongue
but when love comes for you again
my darling, you better not run

this poem is not for you
instead it is for them

I hope you remain a sunflower
and learn to lean on your stem

I hope they lay you down on grass hills
and allow you to make a pillow out of their arm

I hope they never raise their voice
a love that makes you feel safe and calm

I hope they remember your favourite flowers
and hand deliver them to your door

I hope they never eat at the table with you
instead they sit cross-legged on the floor

I hope they kiss you three times on hello
and three more at goodbye

I hope they take you to the beach for sunsets
and hate to make you cry

I hope they go for walks through the trees with you
and never tell you to wear your shoes

I hope they play board games and cards with you
and they know at times to purposely lose

I hope they never grow tired of your accent
and how it will be the sweetest I love you they ever heard

I hope you write them letters
and that they worship every word

I hope they know how much you love your sleep
and to never wake you before the sun

I hope your heart is full
now that you have found the one

I hope you finally make a room for your paintings
and they know when to give you space

I hope that if they don't, you tell them
so they can take you to a quiet place

I hope that from time to time you still think of me
and that I don't sound selfish when you read this

after all, I can set you free
yet still love you unconditionally

FOLD THE CORNER

You leave me like I am always going to be here
I have waited long enough for the dark clouds to clear

I never expected you to travel the whole distance
just meet me halfway
but it is a little too late, yet I have so much left to say

I always believed you and I met for endless reasons
thank you for all the love you gave through the four seasons

it was more than enough, just never consistent
one moment you are here, the next you are distant

reminisce on the memories and just walk with me slow
our story felt familiar, as if it begun a lifetime ago

a piece of you will always be mine, as a piece of mine is yours
so, give me one last smile before we close our chapter
and walk through a hallway of unlocked doors

To the brown eyes and golden smile
who always pushed me to finish what I start
and for the love that would have been memories
only now transformed to art

to my beautiful family
for building my foundation of love
the ones still present with me
and the ones dancing in the clouds above

thank you

www.ingramcontent.com/pod-product-compliance
Lightning Source LLC
LaVergne TN
LVHW010628100826
845148LV00014B/3164

* 9 7 8 0 6 4 5 8 3 3 6 0 7 *